George W. Shaffer

Azilia

A Historical Legend of Georgia, from 1717

George W. Shaffer

Azilia
A Historical Legend of Georgia, from 1717

ISBN/EAN: 9783337242800

Printed in Europe, USA, Canada, Australia, Japan

Cover: Foto ©ninafisch / pixelio.de

More available books at **www.hansebooks.com**

AZILIA.

AZILIA:

A HISTORICAL LEGEND OF GEORGIA,

FROM 1717.

[From Original Papers Published at the Time.]

A LAND OF BROOKS, OF WATER, OF FOUNTAINS;
A LAND OF WHEAT AND BARLEY, AND
VINES, AND FIG TREES, AND
POMEGRANATES,
AND HONEY.

COMPILED BY

GEORGE W. SHAFFER.

SAVANNAH, GA:
EDWARD J. PURSE, PRINTER,
1870.

To the Reader.

———◆———

I publish for the Citizens of Georgia, ''The Historical Legend of this State in 1717.''

Its genuineness may be determined, by reference to published Documents.

Those obtained from the late PETER FORCE, Esq., are with the assent of his Executor.

Respectfully,

GEORGE W. SHAFFER.

Plantations of new countries, says the great Lord Bacon, are among the primitive and most heroic works of man. They are meritorious in a double sense, religiously as they illuminate the souls of heathens, through the darkness of their ignorance, and politically as they strengthen the dominion which sends out the colony and wonderfully more than any other means enrich the undertakers.

Excited therefore by an earnest inclination to establish such a settlement as may by new means, yield new benefits as well as in wealth as safety; and resolving to proceed upon a scheme entirely different from any hitherto attempted and which appears to promise great and inexpressible advantage; the grant on which we found the undertaking will be seen in the following abstract:

The underwritten Palatine and Lords Proprietors of the Province of Carolina, do on the consideration hereinafter mentioned; grant, sell, alien, release and confirm to Sir Robert Montgomery, Baronet, his heirs and assigns, forever, all that tract of land, which lies between the rivers Alatamaha and Savanna, together with the islands, ports, harbors, bays and rivers, on that part of the coast, which lies between the mouths of the said two rivers, to the seaward; and moreover, all veins, mines and quarries of gold and silver, and all other whatever, be they of stones, metals, or any other things found, or to be found, within that tract of land, and the limits aforesaid; with liberty over and above to make settlements on the south side of Alatamaha river, which tract of land, the said underwritten Lords, do erect into a distinct Province, with proper jurisdictions, privileges, prerogatives and franchises, independent of and not subject to, the laws of South Carolina, to be holden of the said Lords by Sir Robert, his heirs and assigns, forever, under the name and title of the Margravate of Azilia, at and under the yearly quit-rent of one penny sterling per acre, or its

value in goods or merchandise, as the land shall
be occupied, taken up, or run out; payable yearly to the Lords Proprietors' Officers, at Charles
Town, but such payment not to commence till
three years after the arrival of the first ships
there, which shall be sent over to begin the settlement; over and above which penny per acre;
Sir Robert, his heirs and assigns, shall also yield
and pay to the Lords Proprietors, one fourth part
of all gold or silver ore, besides the quota reserved to the crown out of the said royal miner-
als; District Courts of Judicature to be erected,
and such laws enacted within the Margravate, by
and with the advice, assent and approbation of
the freemen thereof, in publick assembly, as shall
be most conducive to the utility of the said Margravate, and as near as may be conveniently
agreeable to the laws and customs of England,
but so as such laws do not extend to lay duties
or custom or other obstruction upon the naviga-
tion of either of the said rivers, by any inhabi-
tant of South or North Carolina or their free
commerce and trade with the Indian Nations,
either within or to the southward of the Margravate, Sir Robert consenting that the same duty

shall be charged on skins within the Margravate, which at this time stands charged on such skins in South Carolina, and appropriated to the maintainance of the clergy there, so long as that duty is continued in South Carolina, but the said duty shall not be increased in Azilia, though the Assembly of South Carolina should think fit to increase it there, nor shall it longer continue to be paid than while it shall remain appropriated as at present, to the maintainance of the clergy only : In consideration of all which powers, rights, privileges, prerogatives and franchises, Sir Robert shall transport at his own expense a considerable number of families, with all necessaries for making a new settlement in the said tract of land, and in case it be neglected for the space of three years from the date of this Grant, then the Grant shall become void, anything herein contained to the contrary notwithstanding.

Dated June the nineteenth, 1717.

CARTERET, *Palatine,*
IA BERTIE,
   For the Duke of Beaufort.
M. ASHLEY,
JOHN COLLETON.

A DESCRIPTION OF THE COUNTRY.

t lies about the 31st and 32nd degree of northern latitude—is bounded eastward by the Great Atlantic Sea—to the west by a part of the Apalachian mountains, and to the north and south by the two Great Rivers mentioned in the Grant.

In the maps of North America, it may be taken notice of, how well this country lies for trade with all our Colonies, and in regard to every other prospect, which can make a situation healthy, profitable, lovely and inviting— Florida, of which it is a part, received that name from its delightful *florid* and agreeable appearance.

It has been commonly observed that gay descriptions of new countries, raise a doubt of their sincerity; men are apt to think the picture drawn beyond the life to serve the interest of the representer. To show the prejudice of this opinion, whatever shall be said upon the subject. Here is all extracted from our English writers, who are very humorous, and universally agree that Carolina, and especially in its southern bounds, is the most amiable country in the universe; that nature has not blessed the world with any tract which can be preferable to it, that Paradise with all her virgin beauties may be modestly supposed, at most, but equal to its native excellencies.

It lies in the same latitude with Palestine herself, that promised Canaan which was pointed out by God's own choice to bless the labors of a favorite people. It abounds with rivers, woods and meadows. Its gentle hills are full of mines — lead, copper, iron and even some silver. It is beautiful, with odoriferous plants, green all the year, pine, cedar, cypress, oak, elm, ash or walnut; with innumerable other sorts both fruit or timber trees, grow everywhere so pleasantly that though they meet at the top and shade the traveller, they are at the same time so distant in their bodies, and so free from underwood or bushes, that the deer and other game, which feed in droves along the forests, may be often seen near half a mile between them.

The air is healthy and the soil in general fruitful and of infinite variety: vines naturally flourishing upon the hills, bear grapes in most

luxuriant plenty. They have every growth
which we possess in England, and almost every
thing that England wants besides. The orange
and the lemon, thrive in the same common
orchard with the apple, and the pear tree,
plumbs, peaches, apricots and nectarines, bear
from stones in three years growing.

The planters raise large orchards of these
fruits to feed their hogs with—wheat ears have
been measured there seven inches long, and
they have barley, beans, peas, rice, and all our
grains, roots, herbs and flowers—not to speak of
numbers of their own, which we can find no
names for; beef, mutton, pork, tame poultry,
wild fowl, sea and river fish, are all there plenti-
ful, and most at lower rates, than in the cheap-
est parts of Wales or Scotland.

The many lakes and pretty rivulets through-
out the Province, breed a multitude of geese,
and other water fowl; the air is found so tem-
perate, and the seasons of the year so very reg-
ular, that there is no excess of heat or cold nor
any sudden alterations in the weather—the river
banks are covered with a strange variety of
lovely trees, which being always green, present

B

a thousand landscapes to the eye, so fine and so
diversified, that the sight is entirely charmed
with them ; the ground lies sloping towards the
rivers, but at a distance rises gradually and in-
termingles like hills of wood with fruitful plains,
all covered over with wild flowers and not a tree
to interrupt the prospect. And this tempting
country is not inhabited except those parts in
the possession of the English, unless, by here and
there, a tribe of wandering Indians wild and
ignorant, all artless and uncultivated, as the soil
which fosters them.

OF THE FORM PROPOSED IN SETTLING.

ur meaning here relates to what immediate measures will be taken, for security against the insults of the Natives
during the infancy of our affairs; to
which end we shall not satisfy ourselves with
building here and there a Fort, the fatal practice of America, but so dispose the habitations
and divisions of the land, that not alone our

houses, but whatever we possess, will be enclosed by military lines impregnable against the savages, and which will make our whole Plantation one continued Fortress. It need not be supposed that all the lands will thus be fortified at once.

The first lines drawn will be in just proportion to the number of men they inclose; as the inhabitants increase new lines will be made to enclose them also, so that all the people will be always safe within a well-defended line of circumvallation.

The reader will allow it is not necessary that these retrenchments be of bulk like those of Europe; small defence is strong against the poor unskillful Natives of America. They have accomplished all their bloody mischief by surprises and incursions, but durst never think of a defiance to artillery.

The massacres and frequent ruins which have fallen upon some English settlements for want of this one caution have sufficiently instructed us that strength producing safety is the point which should be chiefly weighed in such attempts as these—Solon had reason when he said to Crœsus looking on his treasure, "You are rich indeed and so far you are mighty: But if any man should come with a sharper steel than yours, how easily will he be made the master of your gold."

At the arrival therefore of the first men carried over, proper officers shall mark and cause to be intrenched a square of land in just proportion to their number. On the outside of this square, within the little redoubts or bastions of the intrenchment they raise light timber dwellings, cutting down the trees which everywhere encompass them. The officers are quartered with the men whom they command, and the Governor-in-Chief is placed exactly in the center. By these means the laboring people (being so disposed as to be always watchful of an enemies approach,) are themselves within the eye of those set over them, and altogether under the inspection of their principal.

The redoubts may be near enough to defend each other with muskets, but field-pieces and patarero's will be planted upon each, kept charged with cartridge shot and pieces of old iron.—

Within these redoubts are the common dwellings
of the men who must defend them; between
them runs a palisadoed bank and a ditch, which
will be scoured by the artillery. One man in
each redoubt kept night and day upon the
guard, will give alarm upon occasion to the
others at their work. So they cultivate their
lands, raise their cattle, and follow their business,
with great ease and safety. Exactly in the center of the innermost square, will be a Fort defended by large cannons pointing every way,
and capable of making strong resistance in case
some quarter of the outward lines should chance
to be surprised by any sudden accident, which
yet with tolerable care would be impracticable.

The nature of this scheme when weighed
against the ignorance and wildness of the
Natives will show that men thus settled may at
once defend and cultivate a territory with the
utmost satisfaction and security, even in the heart
of an Indian Country, then how much rather in
a place considerably distant from the savage
settlements.

As the numbers shall increase and they go as
to clear more space of land, they are to regulate

their settlements with like regard to safety and
improvement and indeed the difference as to the
time and labor is not near so great as may be
thought betwixt enclosing land this way, and
following the dangerous common method; but
what is here already said will show the end for
which it has been written which was only to give
a general notion of the care and caution we pro-
pose to act with. It will not however be amiss,
as you have seen the first rude form of our Azilia
in her infancy, to view her also in the fulness of
her beauty; and to end we have affixed a plan
of one whole district, cleared, planted and inhabited; for as the country thrives, all future
townships will be formed according to this plan,
and measured out as near each other as the
rivers, hills, and other natural impediments will
in any way admit of.

But least it should be feared from the cor-
rectness of this model, that it will be a work
of too great difficulty, and require a mighty
length of time to bring it to perfection, we think
it proper to declare that purchasers will not be
obliged to wait this form of settlement, but are
entitled to the immediate profits of peculiar

lands, assigned them, from the first arrival of
the Colony; which lands being set apart for
that purpose will be strongly enclosed and defended by the lines or intrenchments before
mentioned.

Neither would we have it thought a labor so
tedious as it is generally fancied, to establish in
this manner a Colony which may become not
only an advantage but a glory to the nation.

We have prospects before us most attractive
and unprecedented; in the three tempting
points—wealth, safety and liberty; benefits like
these can never fail of drawing numbers of inhabitants from every corner. And men once
got together, it is as easy to dispose them regu-
larly and with due regard to order, beauty and
the comforts of society, as to leave them to the
folly of fixing at random and destroying their
interest, by indulging their humor; so that we
have more than ordinary cause to expect that in
a very short time we shall be able to present
the solid life itself, as now we give the shadow
only in the following explanation.

You must suppose a level dry and fruitful

tract of land in some fine plain or valley, containing a just square of twenty miles each way, or two hundred and fifty-six thousand acres, laid out and settled in the form presented in the cut annexed.

The district is defended by sufficient numbers of men who dwelling in the fortified angles of the line, will be employed in cultivating lands which are kept in hand for the particular advantage of the Margrave. These lands surround the district just in the lines, and every where contain in breadth one mile exactly.

The men, thus employed, are such as shall be hired in Great Britain or Ireland, well disciplined, armed and carried over, on condition to serve faithfully for such a term of years, as they before shall agree to; and that no man may be wretched in so happy a country, at the expiration of those peoples' time; besides some other considerable, and usual incouragements, all such among them, who shall marry in the country or come married thither, shall have a right of laying claims to a certain fee farm or quantity of land ready cleared, together with a house built upon it and a stock sufficient to improve and cultivate it, which they shall enjoy, rent and tax free during life as a reward for their service; by which means two very great advantages must naturally follow; poor labouring men, so secured of a fixed future settlement, will be thereby induced to go thither more willingly; and act, when there, with double diligence and duty, and when their time expires, possessing just land enough to pass their lives at ease and bring their children up honestly, the families they leave will prove a constant seminary of sober servants of both sexes, for the gentry of the Colony; whereby they will be under no necessity to use the dangerous help of Black-moors or Indians; the lands set apart for this purpose, are two miles in breadth, quite round the District, and lie next within the Margraves' own reserved lands above mentioned.

The one hundred and sixteen squares, each of which has a house in the middle, are every one a mile on each side, or six hundred and forty acres in a square, bating only for the highways which divide them; these are the estates belonging to the gentry of the District, who, being so confined to an equality in land will be profitably

emulous of out-doing each other in improve-
ments, since that is the only way left them to
grow richer than their neighbors; and when the
Margravate is once become strong enough to
found many Districts, the estates will be all
given gratis, together with many other benefits
to honest and qualified gentleman in Great
Britain, or elsewhere, who having numerous
and well educated families, possess but little
fortunes, other than their industry; and will
therefore be chosen to enjoy these advantages,
which they shall pay no rent or other consideration for, and yet the undertaking will not fail
to find its own account in their prosperity.

The four great Parks or rather forests, are
each four miles square, that is sixteen miles
round each forest, in which are propagated
herds of cattle of all sorts by themselves, not
alone to serve the uses of the District they be-
long to, but to store such new ones as may from
time to time be measured out on affluence of
people.

The middle hollow square, which is full of
streets crossing each other, is the City: and the
bank, which runs about it on the outside sur-

rounded with trees, is a large void space, which
will be useful for a thousand purposes, and
among the rest, as being airy and affording a
fine prospect of the Town in drawing near it.
In the center of the City stands the Margraves'
House, which is to be his constant Residence,
(or the Residence of the Governor) and contains
all sorts of publick edifices for dispatch or business; and this again is separated from the City
by a space like that, which as above, divides
the town from the country.

———<:>———

DESIGN IN VIEW OF MAKING PROFIT.

he prospects in this point, are more ex-
tensive than we think it needful to dis-
cover. It were a shame, should we confine the fruitfulness of such a rich and
lovely country to some single product, which
example first makes common, and the being
common robs of benefit. Thus sugar in Bar-
badoes, Rice in Carolina, and tobacco in Vir-

ginia, take up all the labours of their people,
overstock the markets, stifle the demand, and
make their industry their ruin, merely through
a want of due reflection or diversity of other
products, equally adapted to their soil and
climate.

Coffee, tea, figs raisins, currants, almonds,
olives, silk, wine, cochineal, and a great variety
of still more rich commodities, which we are
forced to buy at mighty rates from countries,
lying in the very latitude of our Plantation.

All these we certainly shall propagate though
it may perhaps be said, that they are yet but
distant views; meanwhile we shall confine our
first endeavors to such easy benefits as will
(without the smallest waiting for the growth of
plants) be offered to our industry from the
spontaneous wealth which over-runs the country.

The reader may assure himself, our under-
takings upon all occasions, will be the plainest
and most ready roads to profit—not formed
from doubtful and untried conceits, nor ham-
pered by a train of difficulties, none are more
apt than we to disregard chimerical or rash de-

signs, but it is the business of men's judgment to
divide things plain, from things unlikely.

We cannot think it proper to be too particular upon this subject, nor will it, we suppose, be
expected from us. One example however we
will give, because we would present a proof,
that much is practicable there, which has not
yet been put in practice—we shall pitch on potash, a commodity of great consumption in the
trades of dying, glass-making, soap-boiling and
some others; not that this is the only present
prospect which we build on, but as it is necessary we should particularize one benefit, that
others may be credible.

And here it will not be amiss, if we describe
what potash is, and how they make it; since it
is likely some may have attempted it already in
the forest of America, and miscarried by de-
pending upon ignorant undertakers.

It is not very properly indeed called potash,
not being any kind of ashes, but the fixed and
vegetable salt of ashes, which if mixed with water, melts away and turns to lye. For this reason it is preferred to all other lixivate ashes,
c

foreign or domestick, which not being perfect salts, but ashes of beanstraw and other vegetables, made stronger by the help of lye bear no proportion as to price with potash itself, which is as we said before, the pure salt without any of the ashes.

To procure this salt in Russia, and the countries famous for it, they burn great quantities of oak, fur, burch and other woods cut down when flourishing, and full of sap; the ashes they throw into boilers or huge caldrons full of water, and extract a thick, sharp lye by boiling. They let this lye grow clear by settling and then draw it off, and throw away the ashes left at the bottom. This lye so clarified, they boil again, and as the watery part evaporates apace they supply the waste through a small pipe, from another vessel of the same sort of lye, set higher than the boiler; at last, by a continued evaporation the whole vessel becomes full of thick brownish salt, which being dug out in lumps, and afterwards calcined, compleats the work, and gives a colour to the potash like a whitish-blue, in which condition it is barreled up, and fit for merchants.

Nothing can be plainer or more easy than this practice in our intended settlement. As to the boilers, which have ever been the great and terrifying expense and incumbrance of this work, we shall extremely lessen, and reduce that charge almost to nothing, by some new methods, being an experienced invention wherein we use neither copper, lead, iron, nor other mineral, whatsoever, and (that excepted) there is no material necessary but wood only; for wood cut down and burnt upon the ground affords the ashes—the rivers every where abounding in that country furnishes water; ashes and water boiled together yield the lye; the lye evaporated leaves behind the salt, and that very salt calcined, becomes the potash, and it is packed and sent away in barrels, made and hooped there also.

From due consideration of these circumstances, it appears that this must be a rich and gainful undertaking, in a country where the greatest quantities of timber, and the finest in the world, cost nothing but the pains of cutting down and burning on the banks of navigable rivers; where the enlivening influence of the sun prepares the trees much better for this

practice than in colder climates, and where
stubbing up the woods which cover all the settlement, will give a sure and double benefit; for
first they yield this valuable traffick—potash,
and afterwards leave clear the ground they
grow on, for producing yearly crops of such
commodities as are most profitable, and fittest
for the country.

Thus, having faintly touched the outward
lines, and given some prospect of our purpose;
we proceed to the conditions upon which we
will admit of purchasers.

<hr/>

THE PROPOSAL.

o all to whom these presents shall come.
I, ROBERT MONTGOMERY, of Skelmorley,
in the Shiredom of Aire in North
Britain, Baronet; send greeting:
Whereas, his Excellency the Lord Carteret,
Palatine, and the rest of the true and absolute
Lords Proprietors of the Province of Carolina,
in America, have by their Grant, bearing date

the nineteenth day of June last, bargained, sold,
aliened, released, enfeoffed and confirmed to me,
the above mentioned Sir ROBERT MONTGOMERY,
my heirs and assigns : All that tract of land in
their said Province, which lies between the
rivers Allatamaha and Savanna, and erected the
said tract into a distinct Province with proper
and independent jurisdictions, under the name
and title of the Margravate of Azilia, to be held
of them the Lords Proprietors of Carolina, by
me, my heirs and assigns forever ; and whereas
for better carrying on my design of transport-
ing people, and making a new settlement in the
said Margravate ; I have made and caused to
be published the proposals hereunto annexed.
Now therefore for securing the advantages pro-
posed in the said "Articles to All," who shall or
may subscribe any sum or sums of money for
the purchase of lands and profits in the Margravate of Azilia, aforesaid and shall on their
parts, make good the payments and conditions
mentioned in the Articles. I the above named
Sir ROBERT MONTGOMERY do, by these presents,
to be enrolled in the High Court of Chancery,
in perpetual proof and testimony of the secu-

rity hereby designed to be conveyed, engage, bind, mortgage, assign and firmly make subject, the said Grant Lands, and benefits for making good the uses in the said Articles expressed in manner as at large, hereinunder described; and I do hereby declare and consent, that the instruments signed by my hand writing as recited in the Seventh Article, shall be deemed and they are by virtue of these presents, declared to be a firm and sufficient proof of title to the respective claim therein mentioned to be conveyed by, and upon the security by these presents provided. And I do hereby authorize and appoint DAVID KENNEDY, Esqr., in my absence to fill up and deliver the said instruments with all effectual authority and irrevocable rights of representatives, which by Letter of Attorney, or by any other form or means whatever, can or might be deputed to him. And I declare myself obliged as to the sufficiency of the writings delivered, by such act of the said DAVID KENNEDY, as firmly as if I had in person filled and delivered the said writings; and in case that I Sir ROBERT MONTGOMERY, or my heirs or assigns or any claiming right, or exercising power by,

from or under me, shall at any time hereafter
refuse to submit to the said annexed Articles, or
to any of them, or shall under any unjust pretence whatsoever forbear the cultivation of the
purchasers lands, or consign the annual products arising therefrom or any part of the same,
to any other person or persons, than to the Fac-
tor or Factors who shall be appointed by the
purchasers or to persons approved by them, or
shall refuse or deny admission, residence or oc-
cular satisfaction on the spot to any agent,
whom the purchasers may at any time think fit
to send over for that purpose. In any of these
cases the purchasers shall, by virtue of these
presents (any form of law, usage, custom or
pretence to the contrary notwithstanding) have
a warrantable, and incontrovertible right and
authority, to procure and obtain present justice
to themselves in manner following : that is
to say ; upon such breach of covenant the said
purchasers shall or may, meet upon the sum-
mons of the party injured, or of any other person interested, and by a majority of the voices
present, elect a committee of three; which committee shall draw up a state of the case they

complain of; and present it to me, or my heirs
or assigns, or to any agent acting for me or
them, or any of them in London or elsewhere,
and if within ten days after such presentation
they receive not due satisfaction from such person or agent; they shall leave notice in writing
at the place of his dwelling, or publish in the
Gazette, or other authentick News Letter, that
on some day therein named, they design to lay
the state of their case before the King's Attorney General and Solicitor General, in London,
for the time being, in order to have their opin-
ions whether the fact they complain of, be, or be
not, a breach of any part of the Articles hereunto annexed, that so the said person or agent,
may attend if he shall have any thing to offer
in defence of the matter complained of. And
if upon the question the Attorney General shall
join in the opinion, and give it under their
hands, that the cause of complaint does plainly
appear in their judgments, to be a breach of
the Articles.subscribed to, and such person, as
above described, or some agent acting for him,
shall not forthwith make due satisfaction; such
forbearance to do justice in the case, shall after

thirty days next following the date of the said
written opinion, become an absolute forfeiture
of the Grant, and from thenceforth all lands,
prerogatives, privileges, powers and benefits,
whatsoever held, claimed or enjoyed by virtue
of the said Grant, shall be taken possession of,
for the sole future use of the body of purchasers,
and shall be carried on to their general advantage and according to their orders and directions,
by any person or persons whom they shall
choose by a majority of their voices and send
over to that purpose. And that no possible
let or impediment on my part, or the part of my
heirs or assigns, may in any sort incommode or
prevent the most strict and immediate perform-
ance of this covenant. I, the said Sir ROBERT,
do hereby renounce for myself, and all claiming
from me, all pleas, prerogatives, privileges and
pretences, whatsoever, which I or they, may by
the said Grant, or by any form, custom or mode
of proceeding at law be possessed of, or entitled
to; and I do consent and declare, that when the
written opinion above mentioned of the Attorney and Solicitor General, in London, shall be
produced to the Lords Proprietors of Carolina,

and sent over to their Deputies at Charles Town, and be entered in their journal—it shall stand as a determinate judgment recorded against me or them, after which no appeal shall be lawful, and possession shall be given immediately: that is to say; no other process shall be needful than twenty days' notice from the Governor and Council at Charles Town, above mentioned. From which time forever, if full satisfaction be not made within the said twenty days, as well in the matter complained of, as by payment of all costs and damages sustained by the complainants, the purchasers shall in right of themselves, and by virtue of these presents, possess, occupy and enjoy all manner of authorities, territories and advantages of what kind soever, arising from the Grant above said, and I, the said Sir ROBERT MONTGOMERY, my heirs and assigns shall effectually stand excluded, both in law and equity to all intents and purposes, as if the said Grant had never been made.

In witness whereof, I have hereunto set my hand and seal, this Fifteenth day of July, in the Third year of the Reign of our SOVEREIGN LORD

GEORGE, by the grace of God, of Great Britain, France and Ireland, King: Defender of the Faith, &c.

R. MONTGOMERY.

Annoq : Domini 1717.

CONCLUSION.

It was during the Reign of GEORGE THE FIRST, that the effort was made to establish the Margravate of Azilia. And it was in the Reign of GEORGE THE SECOND, that the King of England in 1732, erected by Royal Charter, into a separate Province from South Carolina, the land lying between the Rivers Savannah and Altamaha, under the name of "Georgia."

And in July, 1732, the Trustees for Establishing the Colony of Georgia, held their first meeting; LORD PERCIVAL qualified himself as President, and after taking the oath, LORD CARPENTER, was chosen President. General JAMES OGLETHORPE sailed from Gravesend, on the 17th of November, 1732, in the Ship Anne, and arrived in Savannah, in February—and Georgia became a British Colony.

* 9 7 8 3 3 3 7 2 4 2 8 0 0 *